LIFE IN THE
COAL HOUSE

LIFE IN THE
COAL HOUSE
THE GRIFFITHS FAMILY

WITH ALUN GIBBARD

y Lolfa

First impression: 2010
© Cerdin & Debra Griffiths, Alun Gibbard & Y Lolfa Cyf., 2010

Cover design: Y Lolfa
ISBN: 978 184771 261 5

Printed on acid-free and partly recycled paper
and published and bound in Wales by
Y Lolfa Cyf., Talybont, Ceredigion SY24 5HE
e-mail ylolfa@ylolfa.com
website www.ylolfa.com
tel 01970 832 304
fax 832 782

The Griffiths Family

the parents
Cerdin and Debra

the children
Steffan, Angharad and Gethin

Contents

1

TO THE COAL HOUSE

IT WAS A Saturday afternoon, just like any other. Cerdin Griffiths, his wife Debra and their three children were at home in Cardigan. Steffan, the eldest, was sat on the floor of the living room watching television. Suddenly, he shouted excitedly,

"Mam! Come and see this!"

But mam didn't want to know. She was far too busy and that was the end of that.

"Mam, you must see this!" Steffan tried again.

But the same reply once again from his mother. After a while, Steffan thought that he should explain why he had tried to get her attention. He had seen an advert on the television asking for families to take part in a forthcoming series on BBC Wales. The whole thing sounded very exciting to him. The BBC was looking for families to live life exactly as it would have been in 1927, and this, for up to a month. Steffan was only 13, but he thought the idea was fantastic!

"Don't be so stupid!" is probably the best way to sum up how Debra Griffiths responded to her son's suggestion.

"Why on earth would you think that would be of any interest to us? Do you really think we could do that? Seriously? We couldn't live for two minutes without electricity, television, the phone and the car. They're not offering us a holiday you know!"

Steffan changed his tactics and shifted the offensive towards his father. His response was more subdued. He didn't say a word and Steffan couldn't work out what his dad thought.

He gave up and carried on with his Saturday afternoon. But the same thing happened two weeks later. The same appeal for families. And the same reaction from Steffan. Once again, he tried to persuade his family and this time he was determined not to take 'no' for an answer. Debra could see how resolute Steffan was and listened to him a little more this time. So did Cerdin.

By chance, the next time the advert appeared

on television, the Griffiths family were all watching.

"What I remember was seeing an old miner walking and putting his lamp down on the cobbles," Cerdin recalls, "it reminded me of some of my family who worked down the pits years ago."

"I remember seeing a man sitting on the toilet with his trousers round his ankles!" eight-year-old Gethin chipped in excitedly.

"Yes, that took me back to my childhood days as well!" Cerdin added, "Our house in Ffostrasol was one of the few left without any toilet in the house. Ours was a shed at the bottom of the garden, made from red bricks, with squares of newspaper on a hook on the wall!"

The conversation went on. And as it did so, the family found themselves unwittingly warming more and more to the idea behind the proposed TV series. Angharad, the only girl in the family, found it difficult to work out her own reaction because her brothers were so exuberant. But it seemed to be one big adventure that soon she too would want to be a part of.

After a lot of discussion, Debra finally agreed

to put their names forward to be part of the series. She contacted the BBC and asked for an application form.

"I only did it because I didn't think we had any chance at all of getting through, and it was a good way of keeping everyone quiet – simple as that!"

Before long, an envelope came through the letter-box. The Griffiths family filled in the application forms and posted them back to BBC Wales. Most of the family thought that they wouldn't hear any more about it. They could now carry on with their lives exactly as they had before Steffan saw the advert.

But the BBC replied. And that was the start of a process that would change the lives of the Griffiths family forever. Debra's wish for a quiet, normal life was about to disappear. They were on the shortlist of the families the BBC wanted to consider for the series.

"That's the last thing we expected." Debra was in a state of shock. "So my next reaction was to hope that we'd fail at the next step. But at the same time, in the back of my mind, I was starting to warm to the idea. Not that I told anyone else at the time, mind you!"

But every family member had started thinking

a lot more about life in 1927. Every now and again, in the most unlikely of places and at the most unlikely of times, a thought would come to mind; "What exactly would life in 1927 be like?" The children started asking more questions too.

"Well, all we could say was that life in our grandparents' house was a lot of fun and maybe we could have the same fun if we would be chosen to be in the Coal House series," was the parents' response.

But, before going any further in the process, every family on the short list was called to an army training camp at Cwrt y Gollen near Crickhowell. Ahead of them was a day of tests and exercises. Debra's reaction was clear enough.

"An army training camp! Why on earth did we need to go to somewhere like that! What on earth were they going to do with us when we got there? There was a strange mixture of total fear tinged with a little bit of excitement going through me at the time."

There was only one obvious emotion on the night before the training day. Panic! Everyone started to have second thoughts. There were a few suggestions that maybe they should pull out. Maybe, someone suggested, a whole day's training was a waste of time for them and the TV company. What if they failed? Could they then handle not being chosen? And, worse still, what if some of them were still keen to go ahead, but others wanted to pull out? What a scenario! Questions turned round and round in their heads.

Friday night was drawing to a close. They would have to decide before bedtime if they were going to carry on with the training day or not. Should they go or should they stay? Debra finally summed up all their feelings.

"Well, we're damned if we do and we're damned if we don't. So we might as well go!"

So early that Saturday morning in July 2007, the family of five left Cardigan and headed towards Crickhowell, near Brecon. There was a difficult day ahead of them at Cwrt y Gollen. They had been told that the television production company were looking for a family who worked well together and got on, not just a collection of strong, colourful personalities.

"There were all sorts of tests to do. Obstacle courses, working puzzles out, things to do on your own and team exercises as well. People were looking at you every minute that we were there. It seemed as if they were watching you even more when we were talking together informally. They no doubt wanted to see how we got on together when we thought that no-one was watching us. And cooking food as they would have in 1927 was a lot of fun mind!"

The idea for the series had come from the television production company Indus and at Cwrt y Gollen they wanted to make sure that everyone chosen to be in the series was suitable and strong enough to live in a house under 1927 conditions. A psychologist was part of the team on the day, there to assess whether the families were strong enough mentally to deal with the rigours of not only living in the past, but having the whole experience filmed as well.

The five Griffiths family members were more than happy to head back Cardigan at the end of their exhausting trial day. Once they got home, it was straight to bed!

When they awoke the following day, there began a period of playing the waiting game. Had they been chosen to be in the proper Coal House series? They waited patiently for the answer. Before long, the phone rang.

Members of the Indus production team wanted to visit the Griffiths home in order to film some interviews. On the day, the five sat on one sofa, with one camera pointing towards them. The series producer asked them some questions.

"They were very strange questions," said Debra, "nothing like what I expected at all. They were about politics and news stories and things like that."

"Yes, they were strange," Cerdin added, "they even asked us what party we voted for and everything."

The producer then stared at them and said,

"We didn't like you…" Five hearts sank as one. Then the producer continued, "…we absolutely loved you!"

'Gobsmacked' was the word circling in Debra's head. The other four were in so much shock that no words came out at all.

"My mind froze straight away," said Cerdin. "Eventually one word came to mind and I can't tell you what it was! I started to panic big time then, about having time off work and all sorts of things!"

"I was concerned too," said Debra, "worrying about the children having to take up to a month off school and thinking about a cartful of other problems. The stupid thing was we discussed all this in detail when we applied. We'd made arrangements to deal with everything as it cropped up. But now it was going to happen for real and all of a sudden everything sounded and appeared so different! And I was scared stiff about the cooking. How would I keep everyone fed?"

It's obvious that the producer and the film crew were a little disappointed with the family's reaction. They expected more jubilation and a look of more obvious delight on their faces. Instead, they got silent looks of shock and bewilderment. After being reassured that the Griffiths family were actually very pleased with the news, the crew asked them to film their reaction once again.

"And this time they wanted us to show that we were happy on the outside as well!"

From that moment on, life would be completely different for Cerdin, Debra, Steffan, Angharad and Gethin.

But they had to keep the good news to themselves for the time being.

"That was quite difficult! Keeping such exciting news quiet from July through to October was a real strain. We weren't supposed to tell even our closest family members, mothers, brothers, sisters, neighbours – no-one!"

But the family did succeed in keeping it a secret. In fact, they succeeded a little too well. One day, Cerdin's sister and her husband were contacted by Indus. They wanted to discuss some details about the Coal House series with them.

"What happened was this," Cerdin explained, "we had to choose some people who could speak on our behalf on the TV series when we were actually in the 1927 house. We'd done that right back in the early days. Indus now wanted to discuss the practical arrangements of that process with my sister and brother-in-law. But we had not told them that we had been chosen! The first thing they knew was a phone call from the production company."

Other family members found out in a rather more public way.

"The first that many members of our family knew about it was seeing the massive billboards on the side of the road. Well, you can't go round to see everyone personally can you? What a shock they all had, on their way to shop in Tesco and there we were, all five of us on a massive poster on the billboard!"

But the publicity machine had only just started to rumble. For the next month, the Griffiths family were in the public eye all the time. They needed to be filmed outside their new 1927 home in order for the series to be trailed on television. They had photographs taken for the newspaper and magazines, and articles were written about them and their forthcoming adventure. Postcards were printed and left in public places in order to draw attention to the series.

"As well as the in-house photos and everything else, many of the other BBC programmes wanted to interview us too," Cerdin explained, "*Jamie and Louise* on Radio Wales, *Hywel a Nia* on Radio Cymru, *Newyddion* and *Wales Today* on television. It was like a fair – and we hadn't even seen the inside of the house yet!"

And then, finally, the big day arrived – the day they had to move in to their new, temporary home: Stack Square, Blaenavon. This area was the heartland of industrial development in centuries gone by. Stack Square was a row of workers' cottages from that period and was now owned by Cadw. The cottages were surrounded by Blaenavon's present-day buildings, shops, pubs, halls, schools and light industrial units.

But in Stack Square itself, there was no connection with that world at all. They were fenced off from each other. Two moments in time separated by a gate and iron fencing.

Three of the cottages had been prepared for the three families chosen to be in the Coal House series. three two-up, two-down cottages. The three families shared one big yard where a pig and ten hens lived. There was one water pump, also shared. There was no sink in any of the cottages. The toilet for the three families was in a brick building at the end of the yard. The garden was to provide them all with the vegetables they needed – parsnips, sprouts, leeks, swedes and potatoes.

When the three chosen families for the series finally stepped towards their 1927 houses, they had to leave all traces of 2007 behind. Everything remotely modern was placed in a box outside their house.

"The car keys, credit cards and money had to go in the box."

"Even my mobile!" Steffan remembered, all too well.

"I had to put my engagement ring in. I was only allowed to wear my wedding ring," is what Debra remembered.

"And worse still," Cerdin added, "I had to leave my pants and socks in the box as well!"

They were now ready. Personal possessions from their 2007 life lay safely in a little box. Waiting for them in a house not much bigger than a box, was life as it was in 1927. The adventure was about to begin.

2

UNDERGROUND

I DRIVE A lorry for a living, delivering oil to people's houses. It's a great feeling to be out and about on the roads, going from one place to another in an area of Wales that's very beautiful and very close to my heart. I was born and bred in Ceredigion and most of my time is spent on the county's roads, meeting all sorts of people at their homes.

It was quite a shock to realise that my work, whilst living in Stack Square would take me right down into the belly of the earth. I had been told before we actually moved in to No. 6, but facing it for real was a completely different ball game.

The reality of working underground started to dawn on me when the woman from the television company came to our house to tell us that we had been chosen. After the bombshell of realising we had been successful had started to die down a little, she turned to me and said, "Of course, you're claustrophobic aren't you Cerdin?"

All of a sudden it was time for me to think about it for myself, not just hear other people talk about it. It was like a switch being turned on in my mind. I had to face the situation now. And in considering that one fact of having to go underground, all sorts of other things started to dawn on me as well. I had to take my family – my wife and three children – away from the life we enjoyed in the time present, back to live life as it was in 1927. Was it really the right thing to do?

What would I tell the boss? That was another problem for me to think about. I would be away for over three weeks. I had mentioned it to him when we made the application. But that was a 'what if' sort of chat. Now it was 'Can I...?' We had been chosen. It was going to happen! What would I tell him? What would his response be? I hoped to goodness he wouldn't say no after we had been accepted.

So many thoughts to consider! Each one going round and round in my head day-in, day-out. Each one fighting for its place to be at the centre of my attention. Life had been so much more straightforward before!

One problem was sorted quite quickly, thankfully. The boss was more than happy to give me the time off. He was really positive about it, to tell you the truth, and that was a huge weight off my shoulders. But there were still plenty of other things left to sort out and one of them was pretty important. The claustrophobia! Well, what a problem! How can a man who's afraid of small, dark narrow spaces go and work in a coal mine?

I decided I needed some practice before going. For some weeks prior to swapping 2007 for 1927, I tried to get my head used to the idea of small spaces in the dark. But not in an actual coal mine, though, as there aren't many of those in Ceredigion! The best thing that helped me was something as simple as changing my habits when I got up in the middle of the night to go to the toilet. Instead of switching the lights on, I started to walk through the house in darkness! Simple, but effective. It didn't cure my claustrophobia of course. It would take a lot more than that. But it was a start.

The first day we moved into the house, there

were so many other new and different things for me to get my head around.

"Dad, what's this?"

"Dad, where's the toilet?"

"Dad, who's sleeping where?"

And then there was Debra's questioning! And the initial biggest challenge of living in No 6 Stack Square? Well, lighting the open fire and keeping it alight. But I'll let Debra tell that story! There was little opportunity to think about my problems for quite some time. By the end of that first day, with so many other things going on, all thoughts of working underground had gone out of my head completely.

But a note placed under the door soon changed all that! The message was simple – all the men were to report for work the following morning.

For me as for everyone else these days, getting up in the morning is a regular routine of turning on the lights in a house which is already warm due to central heating. There's carpet under my feet as I walk to the shower. Breakfast is ready in two minutes and sandwiches for lunch are in the fridge from the night before. The car gets me to work in no time at all and I arrive there bone dry. That was certainly my everyday routine.

But not in Stack Square, 1927! Getting up in the morning in that house meant stepping onto a cold stone floor. It was pitch black everywhere and there was no point trying to fumble for switches because there weren't any. There was absolutely no guarantee that embers from the previous day's fire were still glowing and without a fire there would be no hot water to wash, cook or make a cup of tea! There would never be enough time to warm water up before going to work, so away I would go, just as I was when I got up. I would've hated to have started my day like that before getting into my lorry. The other Coal House men were in the same situation as me, crawling out of bed, straight to work with no creature comforts such as food or warmth.

Debra had to get up at the same time as me, so that she could start to impose some order on the day. It was Debra's job to make my sandwiches for lunch. It was her job to relight the fire if it had gone out too, which she had to do before the children got up. She then made sure that they were ready for school.

Nothing could have prepared me for the journey to work. We had to get up at six o'clock in the morning to walk three miles to work and then, after a hard day's labour, walk the return journey at the end of the day. It's hard to imagine that people had to do that every day of their working lives. What an effort! It wasn't so bad for us for the first few days, to be honest, because there was a certain novelty factor to it. But we soon realised that walking such distances at either end of a shift was quite an effort and quite draining as well! And to make matters even worse, it was October, so the weather didn't give us any particular delight on our way either. Up to that first morning, I'd been convinced that we would be filmed leaving Stack Square on foot and then a car would pick us up once we were out of sight. We would then be dropped off round the corner from the pit and we would have to pretend that we were weary from all our walking as we entered the pit. But there was no pretending at all, believe you me, because we walked the six miles every single day!

In order to walk such a distance to work, we would obviously have to leave the house earlier than we would on a normal working day in our real lives and return home later. A working day was therefore many hours longer than what we were used to.

A man called Mr Blanford owned the colliery

where we worked and it was called Blaentyleri Drift Mine No. 2. It's still a working mine today. In 1927 there would have been 127 drift mines in the area and 30 shaft mines, each one of them working nine seams of coal. Mr Blanford awaited our arrival by the gate every morning – and on the first day we were reprimanded for being late! What a good start that had turned out to be! But there was an even bigger shock for me when he started to tell us about the work we were supposed to do.

The first few days were given over as training days. Here we learnt to familiarize ourselves with the tools and the working practices. We then learned that the coal face was very deep. It was also eighty metres long and it wasn't possible to stand up whilst you worked on the coal face. The worst possible news for me was that the seam was only two foot six in some places. Much of it was three foot six in height, and if we were lucky there would be occasions when we would be able to get up on our knees to work. Well, talk about the fears flooding in!

I felt totally confused and my head was spinning. I didn't know if I wanted to go underground as soon as possible in order to get it over and done with, or wait a while longer in order to get used to the idea. But at the end of the day, it wasn't up to me anyway and before I knew it, I was walking with the other men down into the belly of the earth to cut coal.

I can't say that I was particularly clever at school, but I did remember from my history lessons that working underground was a very dangerous occupation especially in the years before the Second World War. I'd heard some of my family's recollections of their lives down the pit as well. Accidents happened regularly and people got killed. That was in the back of my mind as we ventured underground that first day. But once the work started, the pick and shovel grafting work, there was no time to think of anything else but getting the coal from the rock.

But before we were able to do that, we had to crawl for some fifty metres to get to the seam – before we could even start to think about working.

Not long after, I could hear one voice loud and clear, "Come on Cerdin!" Mr Blanford was shouting at me because he thought I wasn't pulling my weight. I got used to that sound!

Our pay for a day's work depended entirely on how much coal we had dug and put into the drams. We were expected to take out about eight or nine tons a day and for that we would earn ten shillings of pay. However, if we didn't fill the drams, we would take less money home. Mr Blanford kept a beady eye on each one of us. The three men who were in Coal House could potentially earn more or less than the other. That was very difficult to accept when we were in there together, trying to get on as one and on equal terms. In my every day job, every one who does the same job as me gets paid the same as me. But not underground in 1927.

The work was difficult and relentless. We had to hack the coal out of the face, gather it together, and then shovel it into the drams before pushing the drams to the exit, from where they would be taken to the surface. It was extremely physical work with the added mental pressure of knowing that our pay depended on how much coal we produced. That in turn determined the amount of food we could put on the family table. And that's quite a lot of pressure and responsibility.

We only had a quarter of an hour break during each shift. At that point we'd eat our chunk of bread and butter, cheese, a slice of *teisen lap* and a Welsh cake. When times were hard for some of the other men, they would only have bread and treacle to eat. Water was the best thing to drink, but some preferred cold tea, because it was so warm underground. We had to make sure that the food was kept in a box that had a tight lid because otherwise the mice would get at it.

I must say that there was one advantage from working in such a way – strange as it may seem to say so. After some days of working like that, my claustrophobia disappeared completely. There was no time to think about it. You hear of these celebrities going on *I'm a Celebrity, Get Me Out of Here* in the jungle and facing their deepest fears. Well, I did that in Blaentyleri No. 2! Sometimes my mind wandered and I could feel myself starting to worry. I could hear myself thinking, "Hell, there's a mountain on top of me!" But those moments didn't last and the claustrophobia went. What a great feeling!

3

OPENING THE DOOR

I DIDN'T HAVE much to say when I walked in through the door of No. 6 Stack Square for the first time. All I could do was repeat, "Oh my God!" – about a dozen times! I walked around with my mouth wide open. Now and again a different sentence would come out, such as, "We're not all going to fit in here! There's no room for me, Cerdin *and* the children!" It's one thing seeing a house like that in St Fagans or somewhere like that; it's totally different realising that such a place is going to be your home for almost a month.

It was the things that were missing that struck me the most. There was not a single thing that would be familiar to you in a house today – there wasn't even a washing machine for goodness sake! I had to cook food in the fireplace! It soon became apparent that the fireplace was the heart of the household. It was one big black slab in the middle of the wall, and the main focus in the one room where we all had to live during our waking hours – a bit like television is today. And making sure that the fire was kept alight sounded like an easy enough job. No. It proved to be quite a battle actually.

For what seemed like hours on end, the only thing on view was Cerdin's backside, as he knelt in front of the fire, trying everything he could to get one little spark to ignite the fire. He chopped wood, he cut coal, he ripped papers, and he stuffed them in on top of each other in different ways. And as one attempt failed and led to another, he got more and more frustrated and furious.

Then, he would grab the bellow from the side of the fireplace and push it through the bars of the grate. There was a lot of blowing and a lot of air. But from Cerdin, not the bellow! And still no spark! I stood behind him watching. It was too much and I couldn't stop laughing. Luckily, he saw the funny side too and he started laughing. There we were, having ended up in a heap, leaning against each other and the fireplace, totally unable to stop laughing with tears rolling down our faces. I was genuinely afraid that I would wet myself, but luckily I didn't! We wouldn't have had a fire to dry the clothes anyway!

One of us then said, "If we don't hurry up, we'll be having toast for supper now!" And we soon realised that that was a stupid thing to say too because we needed the fire to make some toast!

When we'd calmed down, I took over because I was fed up with Cerdin's failed attempts. I put the same amount of effort in, the same amount of energy. But once again, no spark. Throughout the time I was trying to get the fire lit, Cerdin stood behind me shouting, "Come on baby!" – I don't know if he was talking to me or the fire!

Eventually, some success! And from that moment on, it was obvious that keeping the fire alight at all times was the major task. Whatever else needed to be done, maintaining the fire always had to come first. No wonder I had a childhood memory of seeing old ladies sitting by the fire for hours. There they'd sit, looking out the window whilst stoking the fire at the same time. I didn't begin to understand why on earth they did that until I tried to light that fire at No. 6 in those early Coal House days. Certainly, after living in that house for almost a month, I understand now what they were doing. Keeping the fire was keeping the heat and hot water for the house and food on the table for the family.

It was one thing to realise how important the fire is but totally different to know what to do with it. Needless to say, I found out in a way that still makes me feel ashamed to this day.

When the men had been working hard underground all day, they'd come home expecting their meal to be ready and on the table. Therefore, the meat had to be put in the oven early in the day. That wasn't a problem. I was up at about half past six every morning anyway. So, on that first Monday morning, I put the meat into the oven, which was in a part of the fire.

Having worked hard physically, I have no doubt that Cerdin had looked forward to that meal all day. But when he walked in through the door at the end of his shift, the table was bare.

"Where's the food?" he asked as he walked over to open the oven door. The disappointment on his face was so obvious.

"Sorry Cerdin, but I did everything I could. It's not ready."

"What do you mean? It's been in since this morning!"

The meat was still in the oven but it was pink. It was still pink the day after! It was finally the correct colour and therefore cooked on the third day. A three-day roast!

The problem wasn't just keeping the fire alight, but keeping it at the right temperature for it to do its work as well. Another lesson learnt.

The fuss with the fire made me realise one thing straight away. We are very lucky to live our lives in the way we do today. This was a feeling that would grow deeper as the days and weeks in the Coal House went on.

I noticed that particularly when the time came for 13-year-old Steffan to go underground with his father for the first time. Seeing him go into the working world of the men made me think so much about the parents of 1927. They could not offer their sons any other means of a working life. There were no career options. It was a case of "Down the pit you go, good boy and bring us the money back!" That's what it was like – and that was tough.

It soon became obvious that if both house and family were to function as they should, it was essential to be organised. When we arrived at the house, there was a book on the table to help us understand just how this was done in 1927. Organization was the key to everything! Every week and every minute of every day had to be carefully ordered. And I can tell you now, that was quite a challenge!

According to the book, a typical day in the life of a miner's family went something according to this. Get up at six thirty in order to prepare breakfast by seven o'clock – as long as the fire was still alight of course. Cerdin had his breakfast first, which was usually a slice of bread and a cup of tea, but sometimes he would have porridge and tea. And then he'd go off to work and I'd clear his breakfast dishes away.

It was my turn to have breakfast next, before making the children's breakfast at a quarter to eight. I would wake them up so that they could eat it at eight o'clock. They had half an hour to eat it up and then they would walk off to school.

As soon as they were out of the door, I would clear their dishes away. Once that was done, I got on with the house work until half past eleven, which is when I would have to start preparing the children's lunch. It was expected that the children would have a hot meal ready for them by the time they returned for their dinner break. Once the children were suitably fed, I could have my meal. No sooner had the lunchtime dishes been washed and put away than I would begin preparing food ready for the time when the children came home from school.

Then, I had to start preparing food for my husband, which had to be on the table when he came in after walking home from the pit. There also needed to be enough hot water ready for him to have a bath before eating. Once all this was cleared away, the woman of the house could have some time to eat her meal. No sooner had she done that then the children were ready for supper at about half past seven. It is no wonder that everyone was in bed by ten, fast asleep. That was more or less the order of every day for us at No. 6, although not everything always went to plan, as you've already read!

We also had to get used to the water-pump in the yard outside. The three Coal House families had to share the same pump. And even though there was always clean, fresh water available, it wasn't quite the same as being able to turn a tap on inside the house. There was also quite a bit of pressure on us to use as little water as possible. Therefore, if we could use the same water for more than one job, then so much the better. There was always a saucepan full of water to be re-used close-by at all times throughout the day.

I don't know where to begin telling you about trying to wash clothes! Getting clothes white was a real bonus, in an era when no-one had a clue what whiter than white was. Coal dust is something incredibly dirty, which gets right into the fibres of the clothes. I would have to scrub them for hours with soap and water before putting them out on the line in the yard to dry.

One night, as I was sitting in the house (it did happen sometimes), I heard a strange noise outside. I jumped up and went to see what was happening. Some of the pigs had escaped and had wandered across to the clothes line and were taking the clothes off the line and eating them! What wasn't chewed was unceremoniously dragged around through the mud. As I started to chase the pigs around the yard, trying frantically to grab the clothes at the same time, I could hear the children laughing from inside the pigsty! Rascals!

Not long after that, Cerdin started to impersonate Joe, one of our neighbours, because he had cut his finger and was not allowed to work underground. Cerdin would sit there holding his finger up in the air and make whining noises like Laurel from Laurel and Hardy. It was really funny and the kids were in hysterics. I just couldn't stop laughing and yes it did happen this time – I wet myself! There's another pair of bloomers gone. It would be a day or two before they could be washed and dried – so quite simply, I had to go without for a while.

But that happened before a very special visitor arrived at our house, thank goodness. There was a knock on the door one night when we were all sitting comfortably round the fire.

"Mrs Griffiths, please." A big tall man stood in the doorway.

"Yes," I said, "can I help you?" I had no idea who he was.

"I understand you've got some lodgings here. I'm Mr Michael, the new school-teacher."

Well, I didn't know what to say! Cerdin and I

hadn't even discussed the possibility of having a lodger. And we certainly didn't have any time to discuss it now, as the man stood there in the doorway in front of me. The children's faces were a picture of horror as they thought about the possibility of 'sir' living with us. What on earth was I supposed to do? I tried to buy some time.

"Well, I don't know if we've got room for you. Let us have a think..."

Before I had finished my sentence, Cerdin opened his mouth and blurted, "Yes, there's a spare bed downstairs in the back..."

"Oh, that's marvellous, thank you very much!"

And in walked Mr Michael. We now had a lodger and another mouth to feed. Thank you, Cerdin, I said out loud or something similar at least. I showed our new lodger to his room and he was delighted. The rest of us just sat there with strange looks on our faces all night. One knock on the door had triggered off so many different thoughts and feelings.

At the end of the day, as far as I was concerned at least, we had to balance two different things: extra pressures against extra money. Pressure. Money. Pressure or money.

OK, this time the money won. Seven shillings and sixpence extra every week would be very handy.

So that's how it was. A stranger now lived with us. He was the children's teacher and he didn't speak Welsh. Great.

4

STEFFAN

I WAS THIRTEEN and a half when I went into the Coal House. I was the one who saw the advert first and I desperately wanted to go and live in the house. Many people have asked me since why I was so keen to go back to live life as it was in 1927. It wasn't really much to do with wanting to be on television. That might have been a small part of the reason, but for me it was more to do with wondering how we as a family could cope with such an experience. It looked like a challenge that could also be a lot of fun. It wasn't going to be something that many other people would be able to experience.

One thing that hugely disappointed me almost as soon as we got to Stack Square was that mam and dad decided that I was to go to school with my sister Angharad and my brother Gethin. That was not in my plan at all, because they are both much younger than me and it would be strange to attend the same school. To be honest, before going to No. 6, I set put my mind on working underground. That's all I wanted to do.

There was a 14-year-old boy called Ryan living next door to us. He was allowed to go to the coal mine with his dad, Richie. And that made matters a lot worse. He could go to work with the men, but I had to go to school with the children. My parents and I discussed this quite a lot.

"But it's not fair mam! Ryan is allowed to go and there's only six months between us!"

"Yes Steffan, but his parents have got six children to feed and they need to get as much money as possible in every day. That's why he's allowed to go. And anyway, do you realise how difficult the work is underground, and it's dangerous. No chance, good boy!"

That's how it was for a long time. If I had known before going on the series, I wouldn't have been so keen to do it. But I just had to get on with things as best I could. Thank goodness that Osprey was such a help!

Osprey was one of the hens. We played outside in the yard all the time and playing with the hens was always a great laugh. We all got to know each one of them fairly quickly, and I named my hen Osprey.

Dad went out to feed the hens one morning – and I got my chance to do some mischief! I pushed him in to the chicken coop and locked the door behind him. Everyone came out to hear what the noise was and started laughing as soon as they realised that dad was locked in the chicken coop and was screaming to get out! Leading the fun was mam of course, talking to dad as if he was one of the hens. "C'mon Cerdin, cluck, cluck, cluck...!"

"Let me out you...!" he said, shouting and banging the door frantically as he got more and more worked up. The hens ran away as fast as they could and everyone else walked round the coop banging on the sides to frustrate him even further. He did get out, eventually!

One day the teacher gave us a history lesson about the south Wales coalfield. He read out a story about a horrible accident at the Senghenydd Colliery where over 400 men and boys were killed. He said it was the worst accident in a Welsh coal mine.

"That was only fourteen years ago and only down the road from here. And some of the boys killed were only your age," Mr Michael said, pointing his finger in my direction.

I think he was trying to frighten me so that I wouldn't want to go underground to work. However, his warning didn't work. I still wanted to go down the mine with dad. One day, after thinking things through, I tried a different approach and I think that it made them think again.

"Dad gets ten shillings a shift. I could earn five shillings. That's a lot of extra money for us every week, isn't it?"

They didn't agree straight away, but I had planted a seed. They were beginning to think in a different way. Not long after, the topic cropped up again.

"We've decided, Steffan, that we are going to pull you out of the school and you can go to work with your father."

I was so chuffed! My dad made sure I understood what it would be like to work in a mine, and I was really excited and couldn't wait for that first working day to come.

When the big day dawned, I was up bright and early and eager to start the walk to the pit. Ryan and I discussed it on our walk to work. We talked about the money and what kind of work

I would be doing. It was strange though having to walk to work. Back home in Cardigan, mam would give me a lift if I wanted to go anywhere. Three miles to the pit was certainly going to be an adventure.

If it had been 1927 proper, Ryan and I would have been underground with real miners. But the laws of 2007 wouldn't allow us to do that, so we worked on the surface clearing and separating the coal from the stones. When I received my first wages, they were less than five shillings. After a few days the picture began to change: to be honest, the novelty was beginning to wear off. And yes, I have to admit that, after a while, I would rather have been in school. I thought that I would feel more of a man doing this kind of work. Man's work not school work for children. But it wasn't like that at all. I carried on going to the pit and the money was nice to have. But I think I had what we would call in 2007 a reality check!

5

A TOUGH COALFACE

A T THE END of one shift at the coal mine, we got an urgent message telling us that there had been an accident and that all hands were needed to help with the rescue. One man had been injured and he was trapped under a mound of coal. We were ready to make our way home when we got this message and our wives would be waiting for us with supper on the table and hot water ready for our baths. But, at the same time, I felt quite proud that I was able to help in a rescue. There was no choice really. We had to postpone our journey home and help as best we could. The rescue work was a totally different kind of pressure to what we were used to. The roof of the shaft had fallen down on top of some of the workers. Almost every one of them had been found and brought out safely, but one was missing. Our job was to find him.

We had to use everything that we could find

Our home for the next month: No. 6 Stack Square, Blaenavon. The vegetable patch was shared between the three families. We ate lots of kale, but not that many carrots.

When it rained, the bare earth surrounding the houses got very muddy. The children often had dirty faces and clothes after playing outside.

The shed at the front of the house contained coal and onions!

The outside toilets (one for each house) were cold and dark and not very comfortable. There was no toilet roll, just pieces of newspaper.

Our pets, the chickens – who were all named by the children. Our eggs were very free-range.

Steffan once locked his dad in the chicken coop.

The pigs Salt and Pepper enjoyed roaming and Pepper enjoyed eating Debra's pink bloomers.

The Ironworks which were nearby.

The stark bedroom; no curtains and certainly no *en suite*!

All five of us slept in one bedroom. Debra and Angharad in the single bed and Cerdin, Steffan and Gethin in the three-quarter bed.

The chamber pot was kept under the bed. It overflowed a few times!

Twenty-first century fashion was also left behind.

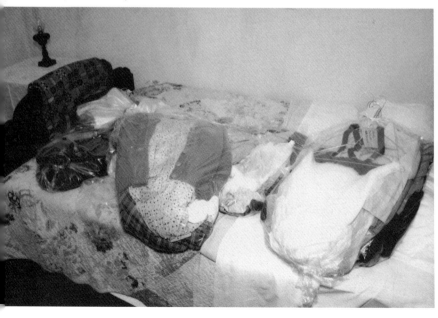

Oil lamps for lighting and plenty of jugs to store water.

A basic, but pretty healthy diet. But we missed eating oranges; we only had two to eat during the whole experience.

Baths were taken in a very small bath in front of the range. Debra just about managed to get in.

The same tin bath would collect water from the pump outside the house.

Washing clothes needed time and elbow grease with the help of a washboard, mangle and dolly.

The entrance to the coal mine and the shovel used by Cerdin to try to extract coal.

The cameras and microphones were everywhere.

After a month of living life as it would have been in 1927, it was time to leave and say goodbye.

It was very sad leaving Stack Square. It had become our little home.

Leaving 1927...

...and through the gates to 2007.

For the Christmas special television programme, we decorated a tree and the house. It was great to go back as it brought back fond memories.

We were joined by a brass band on a bitterly cold night.

We enjoyed singing some Christmas carols!

Cerdin and Debra, happy to be back in Stack Square.

to try and clear the fall of debris. We used every tool that was nearby as well as our bare hands. Work underground pulls everyone together and that had been obvious from my first day there. But looking for an injured fellow miner pulled us even closer together. Someone's life depended on us. There was no time to think about our wives back home worrying about where on earth we were. They must have been thinking all sorts of things. They might well have been thinking that one of us had been in an accident underground or while walking back home in the dark. When we eventually got home, we were told that that was exactly what they had been thinking and that every family had been really anxious about us. But we couldn't dwell on what others were thinking while we had someone to find whose life was in danger. We could only think of the dangers that we were personally facing at that very moment.

"There he is! I can see him – his leg is sticking out, over there!"

We all piled over to move everything that was weighing heavily on him – the coal, the wood, and the stone. We had to be quick, but very careful. When we eventually got him loose, we saw that there was a nasty gash on his leg. We then realised that we would have to carry the injured miner out of the pit to the surface, through narrow uneven tunnels and on a stretcher. It was difficult enough to get ourselves out at times, but now we had someone else to think of. He was a big man. It was quite a strenuous effort to put him on the stretcher and then make our way out to safety. There was a lot of perspiration, heavy breathing, pushing and pulling. And we also had to make sure that we didn't make his injuries any worse.

By the time we eventually succeeded in getting him to the surface, it was extremely late. But after an experience like that, we all knew that we couldn't go straight home. We had to call in for a pint first! So, into the pub we piled, and what a lovely pint we had. A few of us pointed out that our wives would be worrying.

"Forget about your wives!" the landlord said. "You deserve this."

Well, yes, we did actually. Soon, one pint turned into another and another. Before we knew it, we had been in the pub for an hour and a half. Oh dear! We still had to walk home and also had to face our wives, who were not only unaware of why we were late to start with, but would immediately know that we had been to the pub! It would have been impossible to hide the effects of our visit.

"How much did you spend in the pub?" Debra's voice was already ringing in my ear.

It didn't make a blind bit of difference that we had taken part in a dangerous rescue and brought a miner out of the pit to safety. It didn't matter that we had saved someone's life. What really mattered was how much I'd spent in the pub.

The answer was two shillings. That's why Debra's questioning was so abrupt and so loud. I went to bed very quietly that night – no-one was talking to me.

The next morning, everything seemed to be back to normal, thank goodness. We all went off to work once again. But when we got there, we sensed that things were very different. Mr Blanford was waiting for us with very bad news.

"Sorry boys, we've lost an order, no work underground today."

It was like being hit in the face with a shovel. The only work available was maintenance work on the surface and there wasn't enough of that to go around all of us. Richie was the foreman and Mr Blanford asked him to choose either Joe or me to work with him. The person who was not chosen would have to go home. Luckily, he chose me and Joe had to go home.

I felt so relieved that Richie had chosen me, but both of us felt sorry for Joe as well. He'd missed out on a lot of work underground because of a cut to his finger; therefore he'd earned less than Richie and me already. Now he was going to earn nothing at all. I began to feel guilty that I had taken the mickey and impersonated him and his bad finger so much. There was many a time when I had held a bandaged finger in the air and mimicked him pleading for work. That seemed a little out of order now because he had no work at all. Richie and I promised to look after each other at least, and make sure neither of us went without.

The following day, there was an even greater shock for me and Richie. We'd walked to the pit together as usual, but when we arrived there, there was no sign of Mr Blanford. The gate was locked and a sign tied to it said: 'Mine closed. Come back tomorrow.' No work. That was a terrible feeling. We both felt empty but at the same time, we felt a huge burden on our shoulders. How could I tell Debra? How were we going to get food to eat? What about the rent? I started the long journey home to share the bad news with Debra and the family.

When I heard that there was now no work, I took it very badly and very personally. When I left the Coal House, I learned that 24,000 people lost their jobs in south Wales in 1927. My thoughts and feelings would have been very similar to those of men from that time. How many families had faced hardship because of a lack of orders in those days? How many had faced far worse situations than I was now in? But as Richie and I walked home that day, such thoughts were nowhere near our minds. All I could think about was my situation – my wife and my children.

Some time before the work in the pit had disappeared, my son Steffan had started to work with me. He was only 13 years of age. It was a strange feeling to take my son to work with me. It wouldn't happen in normal 2007 life. It wasn't the kind of experience that fathers in the western world had. Even though I thought that it was going to be a good experience for him to walk with us to work, I must say that I had mixed feelings about him working. I knew what kind of work was ahead of him. He might well have been given surface work, but nonetheless, he was in an adult world.

Richie had chosen me and I was grateful for that. But now that the pit was closed, Steffan had to go home with no work and no money too.

All that was left for Richie and me to do at the pit was basic maintenance work. It was just a matter of keeping things ticking over until the orders came back. However, through all this, Mr Blanford's voice kept ringing in my ears. "Come on Cerdin! You've only got half a shovelful there!" He was on my back all the time!

The following morning we headed back to the pit, ready to face another day of maintenance work. But things were progressively getting worse. Mr Blanford demanded money back to compensate for the tools we had used. I didn't have any money, it was as simple as that. But fair play to Richie as foreman, he stepped in and said that he would make sure I would pay for the tools, a little at a time. He gave him his word on my behalf.

The following day, there was still no work. We had walked all the way to the pit only to turn back and go home straight away. The other men and I were not very happy at all. I told Richie that I would like to give Mr Blanford a hiding there and then. There was definitely going to be a difficult time ahead of us now, which would test to the limit how much spirit we had within us. I felt a huge sense of disappointment and failure. I was the one who was supposed to put food on the table. I had no idea how I would react to the lack of money coming in. And however much we told ourselves and each other that it wasn't our fault, there was still a horrible feeling in the pit of my stomach that there was less money coming in to buy food that week and that the pressure of feeding the same number of people on much less money would be on Debra's shoulders.

When pressures like that bore down on us, it was strange how much we thought like people from 1927. Quite often, as we walked to work, we would catch a glimpse of 2007 life, usually in the form of cars passing beneath us in the valley in the distance. I don't remember one occasion when any of us started to think of our 2007 life when we saw those cars. It was quite the opposite in fact. We were such a part of 1927 life that those 2007 cars looked odd and out of place and nothing to do with our world at all. Disasters and hardships were all dealt with and processed in a 1927 way.

One afternoon there was a knock on the door. It was Mr Blanford and two other men from the pit. I had such a scare – I feared the worst. So many men in the pit had lost their jobs. "We're next," was all that went through my mind. Joe, Richie and I were called out to the yard in front of our houses. "Here we go, it's the firing squad," I thought to myself. But thankfully, he brought us good news. They'd had a big order and everyone was needed back at work. Hallelujah!

But what an order! Forty tons of coal needed to be mined in a week. That was forty dram loads, and much more than we had filled since starting at the mine. With such a task in front of us, how would the three of us get on? There was quite a bit of tension between Joe and me as it was. It was all down to how much work both of us could actually do. Joe wanted to prove himself because he'd lost so much work after cutting his finger. But Joe and I were also older, with both of us in our forties. In the real 1927, we wouldn't still be working in the pit at our age. Twenty years or more of working in such circumstances, in small, dark, damp, dusty spaces would have left its mark on our health.

We both wanted to prove ourselves. With so much work ahead of us, there was one thing for certain – we would be tested to the full.

In the middle of one shift and having moved coal as if there was no tomorrow, I was foolish enough to ask Mr Blanford if I could have a break. The teasing afterwards never stopped. "Any excuse not to work, Cerdin!" And Joe, who was older than me, looked across extremely pleased that it was me and not him who had asked for a break.

But seriously, failing wasn't an option. The three of us worked really hard, nonstop and it certainly pulled the three of us closer together. We became a team and bonded really well. Halfway through one shift we were singing hymns at the tops of our voices underground.

Other miners worked at Blaentyleri No. 2 at the same time as us. They were 2007 miners working with 2007 methods. At first, they weren't too sure what to make of us. After all, we were there to make a TV series. They might have thought that we didn't have a day's work in us, and that the whole thing was set up to play to the cameras for a laugh. But at the end of the week, when we had managed to cut 40 tons of coal, we had succeeded in changing their minds.

The three of us gave everything we had in those last few shifts. We had totally bought in to the idea of having to meet a target and that became the most profitable period for us in the mine.

We felt very proud when we heard the other miners, the real miners, say that they had accepted us as equals. We were even more proud when we heard Mr Blanford say to us, "You can deservedly call yourselves miners now!"

When you come from south Wales, a compliment like that is so much more than just words to say that you've done well. It links you with a group of very special men.

6

GETHIN

I WAS THE youngest one in my family in the Coal House series. I was only eight years old when we went into the house in Stack Square and I had absolutely no idea what to expect when we got there. 1927 was so far back in the past for me, I couldn't begin to think what things would have been like then. It sounded like the type of place that Dr Who would have visited!

"Where's the toilet?" was my first question. I couldn't see one anywhere! My dad bent down and picked up a potty from under the chair and said, "This is your toilet!" I could not believe him. We only had two potties between five of us in the house. One day, I remember hearing screams downstairs in the living room. Some people were laughing but not all of them. Water was dripping on top of someone's head in the room downstairs. It seems that someone – but I can't possibly say who – had peed upstairs and missed the potty and it had all gone through the cracks in the ceiling and dripped on top of those downstairs.

There wasn't much room to run around and play in the house. The house was so tiny. So I had to amuse myself in other ways. One day, for some bizarre reason, I decided that I wanted to sleep under the bed. But I'm glad I didn't, because we all shared the same room. Dad, Steffan and I slept in the double bed and mam and Angharad slept in the single bed. And the reason for this? Well, it was a lot warmer like that. And I also think that maybe some of us were a little bit scared at the beginning of the experience as well, to be honest. Dad, Steffan and I had thick stripey pyjamas. And before we went to sleep, we'd all shout good night to each other in the dark. "Good night, love you mam, dad, Steffan, Angharad!"

On that first morning, it was horrible to wake up in a house that was so cold. Everything was dark and miserable. I fell down the stairs on that first morning as well because I wasn't used to finding my way about the place – and anyway, we live in a bungalow in Cardigan!

In the houses next door to us, there were two other families. There were two girls in one of the houses and they were older than me. In the other house there were six children and some of them were younger than me. It was great to have so many children in Stack Square. There was always plenty of company. The chickens were good friends too – I had my photo taken trying to catch one of them!

After we settled in, we had to go to school and every one of us was taught in the same class. We all had our own desks and we sat facing the front – that's where the teacher stood to teach us. But what was most strange was having lessons in English. That made things very difficult for me. On top of that, the teacher Mr Michael was very nasty to us. He shouted a lot and was very strict. He was the man who lived with us also. But thankfully he behaved very differently in the house to what he was like in the classroom.

In one lesson, we were reciting our 'tables' – that's what the teacher called them. I'd never done anything like that before. He turned to me and asked me a question. "Gethin, what are five times five?" I just froze. Then I looked down at my fingers and started to count. I thought there might have been a chance to find an answer that way. He shouted back at me, "Don't use your fingers boy, or I'll chop them off!"

When I got home after school, I cried my eyes out because he had said that. But of course the teacher was coming back to our house for his tea as well. I was crying and he was in the same room as me, which made things ten times worse. I really didn't want to go back to school the following day, but my mam said that I had to. She said that I would get used to the way they did things in 1927. I didn't mind the way we lived life in the house; it was different and I enjoyed it. But school, well, that was a terrible experience.

But then something totally unexpected happened – I became ill. I'd been unwell when we first moved in to the Coal House and I'd been sick a lot. I remember my mam complaining that she couldn't get the clothes clean because the sick had left marks on the clothes. But this time I had chicken pox. Every one thought that that was really funny because I spent so much time with the hens!

But I didn't think it was very funny having chicken pox. Before I went in to the Coal House, some of the other children in my school class in Cardigan had come down with chicken pox. And because we knew then that we were going to go on the television programme, my mother had kept me at home just in case it stopped us going on the series. And believe you me, I didn't complain!

Everyone thought that the plan had worked for a while because there was nothing wrong with me. But I did get chicken pox and it was horrible. I would toss and turn non-stop in bed. I was crying all the time. And to make it even worse, I couldn't play with the other children at all – nor with the chickens either.

My mam kept giving me lots of hugs and she sang to me all the time. But she did do one thing that I wasn't too happy about. She liked to pick my spots! She wasn't very rough but I was worried that she might pick a bit too much and leave marks on my back.

And I really wasn't happy when everyone had a night out in the cinema as a special treat and I wasn't allowed to go. My mam had to restrain me in the bedroom, as I was kicking and screaming because I wanted to go with everyone else to see a film. When everyone returned, Steffan said that it had been a silent movie and no-one on the screen was talking. Instead, a man at the cinema played a piano as background music to the film. How really weird! In the end, I was glad that I didn't go, even though a night out with everyone would have been fun.

I began to enjoy the porridge we had for breakfast each morning. When we entered the Coal House, I asked if there was anything else I could have for breakfast. My mam had replied that No. 6 wasn't a café and that in those days people ate what was available. The first porridge was horrible. No taste at all – it was like eating glue! But I learned that adding sugar to it was a big help and from that moment on, I put a large dollop of sugar on top of the porridge every time I ate some.

7

THE BIG FOUR-O

I'M GLAD TO say that the oven and I became good friends after a few days. I worked out what was what pretty soon, thank goodness, and food was ready to eat when it was supposed to be. Cerdin's meal was on the table when he came home from the pit and the children's lunch was organised for when they came home from school at midday. Imagine my shock, then, when Cerdin came in through the door at the end of one day, carrying a bundle of newspaper parcels in his arms. The children understood straight away. "Hooray! Brilliant! Fish and chips!" the three shouted as one. My heart sank. I held my head in my hands in despair. Then I started to speak my mind.

"For goodness sake Cerdin! What on earth's the matter with you, man?" Nobody could understand my reaction. They all looked baffled.

"We walked miles out of our way to get these as a treat," Cerdin explained, totally confused as to why he had to explain himself in the first place. "Look how much you get, it's an absolute bargain, woman!"

"And I've worked hard all day to do this stew for us all too. And I've cooked some sausages! How could you do this to me?" The children didn't care what I said. They were tucking into their fish and chips by then. "It's a miracle! It's a miracle!" Angharad kept on saying. She made it sound like the feeding of the five thousand with a few loaves and fish!

"The stew you made will keep until tomorrow." Cerdin tried his best to be helpful.

"But I've got bacon for tomorrow!" I must say that even though I could understand why he had bought the fish and chips, I was very upset. In the end, I turned to him and shouted, "Yes OK, but why didn't you phone me then to tell me what you were...?" I realised before the end of the sentence what I'd just said and burst out laughing, as did the others. From then on, I just carried on enjoying the fish and chips like everyone else!

One very real challenge in trying to live as people did in 1927 was the effect it had on

Cerdin and I as husband and wife. We were a married couple from 2007 going into the house, but once there we had to live like a couple from 1927 for almost a month. Interesting, that's all I can say!

What a man was expected to do and what a woman was expected to do were set in stone in those days. And it was completely different to how things are today. For example, as wives, we never went out of the house or to the yard before our husbands. From the minute I got up in the morning to the minute I went to bed, everything I did had to revolve around everybody else. Cerdin was out all day. By the time he'd washed and eaten after coming home from work at the end of the day, he was good for nothing – and I mean good for nothing!

I remember having a chat with Stephanie Phillips who lived next door but one to us. The two of us were on the doorstep chatting one morning, after the men had gone to work. For some reason, we got round to talking about how we both got on with our husbands while we were in Stack Square. "Well, I think he's kissed me once or twice before setting off to work!" I said. "It's all those layers I'm sure!" Stephanie replied.

I knew exactly what she was talking about! It would probably have taken over half an hour to take every stitch of clothing off. Everything was so long and thick! It certainly wasn't worth doing all that for the sake of a few minutes of frolicking!

"And, as well as all that," I added, "what about all those children in the house, and I've got a lodger! How on earth they managed back in 1927, I honestly don't know."

I remember coming down one morning after a little bit of 'how's your father', and Mr Michael was standing by the fire. Well, I didn't know what to say! I asked him if he'd heard any noises in the night, without being too obvious, I hope. "No, no," he said, politely enough. But the little smile at the corner of his mouth suggested he knew exactly what had been going on. I was so embarrassed!

"They would have had lodgers regularly back then and loads of children," Stephanie added, "The two-up, two-down would have been full to overflowing. Where did they get the time to look after so many children, yet alone have the peace and quiet to make them? But then again, as our little handbook tells us, if the man wants it, the woman has to give it to him!"

An added complication for us of course was the fact that there were cameras everywhere. One day, I could hear the sound of furniture being dragged across the upstairs floor. I ran up and saw that Cerdin was dragging the wardrobe forward so that it blocked the camera's view. Brilliant! Until that is, I told Richie Phillips, the next-door neighbour but one. "Oh, you don't have to do all that; I just put my cap over our camera!" But there we are, the end result was the same for both methods.

I didn't even get a kiss on what was a very special day for me in the house. I had my fortieth birthday while I was there. That morning, the men went off to work as normal, and, fair play, the two men in the other Stack Square families gave me a birthday peck as they passed. But did my husband? Did he heck! Nothing. He stood in the yard outside the house, turned round to wave at me and, as he walked off to work, said sarcastically, "Have a nice day, darling!" and "I hope my supper will be ready when I get home!" with a broad smile on his face. But to be fair, he did make one special effort before the day was out, but I didn't know that at the time.

I must say, that was the best birthday I'd ever had. There were only three families living in

Stack Square, and we were all put there to make a TV series. There was a close spirit between us, which turned into something very special on my birthday.

Without my knowing, the children of the three families had been preparing a surprise for me for a few days before my birthday. On the morning of my birthday, each child brought a birthday card they had made themselves to my door. Each one had a different message, and was of a different shape and colour. The first card was from Katie and it said, 'Happy Birthday 1927'. As things turned out, the children couldn't go to school that day either, because the boiler had broken down. It was really nice to have them all at home.

"Where's the birthday girl then?" said the veg-cart man! "What's it like to be forty then?"

How did he know I wonder? But he still didn't forget that he was a business man, birthday or not. He did his best to take advantage of the opportunity.

"Do you want to buy some sweets today, Debra? Two pennies for a bag or five pennies for chocolate. Which one are you having?"

Well, it had to be chocolate. A treat for me to enjoy during the day. That's what chocolate or sweets were in those days, a treat for special occasions. And that day, I had my excuse.

At the end of the day, the men came back from their work, and as on every other day, Cerdin's food was on the table waiting for him. No such thing as a rest – special day or not – it was life as it always was. But there was one exception. Cerdin had the closest thing to a bath that any of us had had since we moved into Stack Square.

"I had to make a special effort for Debra's birthday," Cerdin said as he took his shirt off in the middle of the square, near the water pump. "The water was freezing! But it was a lovely feeling to have half a bath like that. And what a fuss it caused on the Square! Everyone peeping through the curtains and laughing at me standing half naked by the water pump!"

But I had to do one thing to help Cerdin – something unusual that I'm not sure to this day why on earth I did it. I washed his ears. On my fortieth birthday! There I was, scrubbing flat out to make sure that his ears were shining. I had never done that for him before. And what did he say when I'd finished? "I've never had so much love from her in all my life!" What a cheek!

He pulled out all the stops that day. As soon

as he got back in the house, he started to shave with a cut-throat razor. Now I know why they're called that. It very nearly happened to Cerdin – there was blood everywhere and cuts all over him. But he did make that special effort for my birthday, fair play to him.

When we'd all had supper as usual, we got together to celebrate the birthday. All of us were in the Cartwrights' house, which was an achievement in itself, as the houses were so small. But I'll never forget that night.

The children gave me their presents, all made by them during the days in the run up to my birthday. One was made from candle tapers and another was made from wheat stalks twined together. Someone had embroidered one gift, which said 'Happy Birthday'. This was exactly the kind of thing that communities did before TV – as, of course, was the case in 1927.

The fact that they had all put so much thought and effort into what they had done and had come together to organise and do everything was very special to me. Some had been cooking as well, and a nice big cake with 40 on it was pulled out of the oven as soon as we arrived. Even though it was a difficult time for us all, that didn't affect the celebrations. There was no holding back! There was plenty of freshly prepared food and home brewed beer to help us celebrate.

Luckily, there was also a piano in the Cartwrights' house and their two girls and my Angharad started to play the piano and we all joined in with the singing. Well, I could feel the tears welling up inside.

Angharad, Gwen and her sister sang 'Seek ye first the Kingdom of God and His righteousness', and their beautiful voices filled the little room. Everyone took their turn to sing something until the voices of all fifteen of us were bouncing off the ceiling and carrying out through the windows into the distance. 'Calon Lân' (Pure Heart) in particular was really special. Although none of the other families spoke Welsh, everyone did their best to make sure the night was as Welsh as possible, which meant a lot to me.

By the end of the night, I repeated one phrase several times on camera, "I wouldn't have it any other way!" That was so true. It had all been made possible because of three families coming to live together in the Coal House. The television production people talked about our 'natural creativity' emerging that night; everyone using their imagination to make things with their own hands and create a night to remember.

It was enough to bring tears to my eyes. A birthday to remember! And, to cap it all, I had a kiss from Cerdin as well!

8

ANGHARAD

I WAS TWELVE years old when I went into the Coal House and, being the only girl in our family, it was very difficult at the beginning – I didn't like it at all. I'll never forget the first day when we walked into the house. I walked around it very slowly (and that didn't take long), looking at everything very carefully. I couldn't believe my eyes at how strange everything seemed. I was absolutely speechless.

Was this where I was going to live? I was really curious to see how things were going to work out and how we were going to be able to adapt to living there. Everything changed fairly quickly with a mini-crisis on the very first day. All I did was ask my mam for a glass of orange squash. "We haven't got any squash here, Angharad fach. Water from the pump outside is all you'll get now."

I remember that answer so clearly and I honestly thought it was some sort of joke. My mam is very good at teasing us and that's what I thought she was doing at the time. So I didn't pay that much attention to what she'd said. But as time went on, it became obvious that she meant it and was telling the truth. It was the pump outside or nothing – no way!

I only like drinking squash. So it was very difficult going through a whole day without having my favourite drink. Surely that wasn't possible – I had never faced a situation like this before. But, in the end, I just had to accept that my mam was telling the truth and get used to the fact that squash wasn't going to be an option in our 1927 home. I reacted to this news pretty badly. I threw myself on my bed and lay there, refusing to come down stairs at all. I didn't want anyone to come near me. "Angharad, food's ready!" Mam shouted from downstairs, but I ignored her and resolved to stay on my bed for the foreseeable future.

Maybe you think that not being able to have squash is a small thing really. But it was this small thing that made me realise how much our lives had changed. It was the squash incident that made it hit home. I stayed pretty quiet for a few days, but there was no way I could go without food for very long. So I gave up that part of the protest pretty quickly!

The other way I showed my annoyance was by refusing to do jobs around the house. When the series was on television, it showed everyone doing different things to help. I remember Gethin sweeping the floor and me stubbornly sitting on a chair as he swept around my feet.

"C'mon Angharad. You have to do your share!" I remember my mam telling me that loads of times. It wasn't that I didn't want to help. I'm more than happy to do that usually, and in normal circumstances. But everything was too different now. The changes were too much.

But as I said, I got over that after a few days. One thing that helped me a lot was the fact that there were children in the other two families too. We had to live and play together in Stack Square. Our only playground was the yard in front of our cottages, but that was more than enough. We were outdoors all the time from morning till night (if there wasn't any school). It was really funny because each one of us was dirty all the time. We wouldn't be allowed to be that dirty back home! I wouldn't want to be anyway – but it was different here.

The hens and the pigs were important to me. At one time, there was a problem because the hens weren't laying the amount of eggs they should be. Some were laying and some weren't, but we didn't know which were doing what.

"Angharad, come here," Gethin whispered to me one day. "I think I know which hen is laying the eggs." I went over to him, really excited. After watching for quite a while, I realised that it was Gethin's adopted hen that was laying all the eggs. I followed her in to the storehouse where all the animal foodstuffs were kept and saw that she had laid four eggs. Good news for us as a family, because we 'owned' the only hen that was laying eggs.

In a quiet corner near one of the coal sheds, I told this story to the camera, whispering it quietly from beginning to end so that I didn't disturb the hens. And, of course, I didn't want the others to hear where I'd found the eggs! Then, quietly again, I showed the eggs to my mam and told her the whole story.

We needed to work out what to do next. Should we keep the four eggs or share them with the other families? For half a second I was happy for us to keep the eggs. But it was obvious really that the right thing to do was to share them. It was a nice feeling to be able to go to the other families and give them an egg each. But, when you think about it, there was no way of sharing four eggs equally between three families, was there? So no prizes for guessing who got the extra one!

School was strange also. I didn't like the school building or the class. Everyone sat in a row on their own hard chair behind a desk. Very odd! We weren't allowed to choose our seats either. Mr Michael told us all where to sit. Maths was my worst subject – in fact, I hated it. Dealing with the different money that they had in those days was hard enough. What is a shilling anyway? Why did we need to put the letter 'd' after a number when talking about money? English wasn't quite so bad. I understood that better and had a mark of 85% once and that was a nice feeling.

I think two things have stayed with me from my time in the Coal House. The first is the number of opportunities I had to sing. I sang with the Cartwright girls around the piano on my mam's birthday. I sang as well at the special concert we had, and I loved singing in the Diary Room. That was where we would go to say how we felt about things in general, a little bit like

Big Brother's Diary Room – but *we* didn't have a big voice calling us to go in there! One time, I went in there and just sang a song in Spanish from beginning to end without speaking a word to the camera.

But the thing I'll remember more than anything else is the friendships I made with the other children. I'll remember that for a long time to come.

9

BACK IN THE TWENTY-FIRST CENTURY

So that's the Griffiths family story in their own words. But there's one chapter left to be told.

Suddenly, twenty-six days of living in 1927 had come to an end for the Griffiths family and the other two families resident in Stack Square. For Cerdin, Debra, Steffan, Angharad and Gethin, it was time once again to start thinking about moving back to Cardigan and the twenty-first century. Despite the fact that each one of them, in their own way, had found it difficult to adjust to 1927 life, their departure from Stack Square was certainly not going to be easy either.

"It was our home for almost a month," is how Debra summed up the situation. "It was our house, our home. We had a strong feeling of belonging during the weeks we lived in the house."

"That's so true," Cerdin added. "I don't think that any one of us had anticipated going through the experiences we actually did go through. I remember standing in that downstairs room with Debra, in those first few days after moving into No. 6, trying to work out what on earth was in a jar on the table. She didn't know if she had to cook what was in the jar, eat it, or use it to feed the hens. But that was the least of my worries. All I could do was gaze around the room slowly, looking from one object to another in total disbelief, repeating phrases like, 'It's a nightmare come true. I can't believe it. I've never seen anything like this before!' over and over again. By the way, that jar was full of hops, and Debra had to make some home brew with them. But neither of us had a clue what it was at the time."

But Cerdin's worries soon disappeared and he and the rest of his family very quickly threw themselves into their new life. But leaving that life was going to be very difficult now.

Before returning to the present, there was just one more thing to do. They all donned their Sunday best clothes and went to a special concert that had been arranged in the village. 1927 had been the year of the south Wales hunger march, when 400 Welsh miners marched to London to protest to the coalmine owners about the conditions they faced in the pits. Concerts were arranged throughout south Wales to help the miners raise the money to travel to London.

The men from the three families in Stack Square, and the two teenage boys, were given permission to join a male voice choir that took part in the concert. The other choir members warmed to the new recruits, even smuggling pieces of chocolate and sweets to Cerdin and the others without the television production company finding out – until now, that is!

The concert was held in a chapel in Blaenavon. In front of a substantial congregation, the children sang 'Ar Hyd y Nos' ('All through the night') together and then recited some Welsh poetry. The male voice choir stood in the gallery of the chapel, with Cerdin and Steffan proudly taking their places in their midst. Posters were displayed all around the chapel, displaying slogans such as 'Struggle or Starve' and 'Poverty Kills'. That was the spirit of 1927.

At the end of the evening, the choir sang 'Hen Wlad fy Nhadau' ('Land of my Fathers') and everyone became very emotional. Debra was in tears outside the chapel, and Cerdin turned to the camera and said, "I don't want to return to the present day. I didn't want that wonderful concert to end!"

But the concert had to come to an end, and so too their time in Stack Square, Blaenavon in 1927. The three families left their houses for the last time and walked out through the gates which had locked them in for almost a month. Outside, a crowd had gathered to cheer them and welcome them back to the present.

But the surprises hadn't come to an end just yet. There were cars waiting to take the families from Blaenavon, though they had no idea where. But as they drove up a wooded drive, they soon realised that they were being taken to the luxurious Celtic Manor Resort in Newport. However, even after arriving at the hotel, Debra still didn't quite understand what was going on.

"Once we got out of the cars, everyone started walking towards the main door of the hotel. I shouted to Cerdin, 'No, we're not supposed to go in that way, there's a red carpet there for special guests.' So I walked towards a side door. But then I realised that the red carpet was for us! I hadn't seen a carpet of any colour for a month!"

"After we'd gone in through the correct door, it was simply one shock after another," said Cerdin, recalling the buzz surrounding the evening. "To start with, the foyer at the Celtic Manor was bigger than any space I had seen since going into the Coal House. It was as big as all the houses in Stack Square put together. But the biggest shock was seeing that all our families had been invited there too. Talk about the emotion! It was hugs and tears all round!"

The television production company wanted to give the Stack Square families a good time following their challenging 1927 experiences. It was also an opportunity to show some of the footage that had been filmed during the previous weeks, and to ask those last few questions about life in the Coal House. Debra remembers one question more than any other.

"I couldn't believe my ears. The presenter asked me, 'Tell me Debra, what's this about shushi grubi?' I wanted the floor to open up and swallow me. I said, 'I'm sorry, but that's private between me and my husband.'

'Well, not any more – the whole country has shared your secret for the last few weeks. Tell us more!'

Well, I didn't know where to put myself. Shushi Grubi was our phrase for enjoying each other's company as adults, if you know what I mean – it's a secret code. I didn't expect it to be a secret code between Cerdin, myself and thousands of viewers throughout Wales!"

The families and guests then watched a programme from the series. Despite being filmed all day, every day, the families hadn't, of course, seen any of the footage of themselves. It was a strange experience for each and every one of them. Cerdin had not seen anything of the life that Debra had led whilst he was underground. Neither parent knew anything about the children's experiences at school. The Griffiths family didn't know how the other families had spent their time either. There was so much more to learn! "The programme we saw at the Celtic Manor was certainly an eye-opener," said Cerdin. "I had absolutely no idea what the others had been through. It was one thing to hear their stories at the end of the day, but it was something else to see it for myself on a television screen."

Something else was going through Debra's mind as she sat in the luxury of the Celtic Manor, in the midst of families, friends and strangers.

"It was strange getting used to seeing yourself on the box, because we didn't think much about that while in the house. The difficulty *there* was getting used to the camera crew going back and forth. But sitting at the hotel, with the others, it was really strange to watch yourself on screen. It wasn't the excitement of being on the television that hit us that night, but seeing with our own eyes what we as a family had experienced over the previous month in the Coal House."

There would be more of those feelings when they returned to Cardigan, but for the time being, they just got on with enjoying their party.

Thankfully, there weren't too many other surprises that might have caused embarrassment that night. It was a fantastic evening, what with the presence of family and friends making it all the more special. But there was also one more adjustment to be made. The Griffiths family found it difficult to suddenly adapt from the poverty and simple living of 1927 to a sumptuous feast at one of Wales' top hotels. One thing in particular played on Debra's mind.

"I stood there surrounded by hundreds of

people eating and drinking and I couldn't help thinking, 'What a waste!' So much of that food and drink would be thrown at the end of the night. Our day-to-day life in the Coal House had been so different. We had to cut the bread extra thin to make it last, and we often had to go without basic things because we didn't have any money to pay for them. I don't think that I would have ever thought in that way had I not gone into the Coal House. I wasn't back at home yet, but the experience was already having a huge influence on the way I felt about things."

To Debra, it seemed that the world of the Celtic Manor was more unreal than going back eighty years in time to live. But it was something far more practical that struck the youngsters, as Angharad explains.

"I could hardly eat any of the food. Not that there was anything wrong with it, but it was as if my stomach had shrunk over the past few weeks, having got used to eating in the way they did in 1927."

The Griffiths family spent that night at the Celtic Manor – Debra and Cerdin's bed looked bigger than the living room in Stack Square. The following day the family headed back home to Cardigan.

"After sorting through a pile of mail, there was only one thing on the minds of all of us; we had to sit down and watch the whole series. We watched the DVDs of every programme." And for Cerdin, this is when all the pieces started to come together.

"That's when I started to make sense of everything. I couldn't take my eyes off the screen. There were times, mind you, when I had to get up, walk away and have a break before seeing any more. Sometimes it got a bit too much." One incident in particular came back to Cerdin as he remembered having to get used to the cameras.

"Right at the start, there was a shot of me carrying the potty that was under the bed across the yard to empty it. It's embarrassing enough to carry a potty, anyway and it's difficult enough getting used to a camera watching you as you walk. Going through both things at the same time was just total embarrassment. That's obvious when you see it on screen and see the way I reacted. I felt extremely self-conscious. I said something like, 'This is water from our bodies!' And, after emptying it into the outside loo I said something else stupid to the camera, 'They're lucky it's number ones. No way am I carrying number twos!'"

Even though there were cameras everywhere in Stack Square, it was obvious that Cerdin did manage to relax and get used to them eventually. And whilst watching the DVDs back home in Cardigan, he realised that he may have said some things that he shouldn't have.

"When I was describing the job that I normally do (that is, delivering oil), I said on camera that if I finished everything early, I would have a little snooze in my cab in the afternoon. I don't think that went down well with the boss when he saw it! What a stupid thing to say." And there was something else that Cerdin hadn't realised that his boss would see.

"In one shot, I was about to have a bath after coming home from a shift in the pit. I walked from the living room to the back bedroom completely naked. Everyone saw everything – from the back, thank goodness! Well, when I saw that, I started to think of all the people who'd seen me like that, people I would have preferred hadn't. And my boss was one of those!"

Debra had quite a surprise when she saw the Coal House website.

"It was a huge shock to see how many people had contacted the website and left messages. It was hard to believe that we, as a family, had been part of something so many people wanted to watch on TV when they were relaxing at home. That's quite something to take in. It was rather shocking, but also quite amusing, to see so many references to shushi grubi! People left messages like, 'We're doing a Debra and Cerdin now – it's shushi grubi time!'"

Debra was struck by just one unpleasant thing, namely Gethin's experience in school.

"That was the hardest thing for me, without a doubt. When I saw the teacher shouting at Gethin, 'Don't use your fingers to work the sum out or we'll chop your fingers off,' I nearly screamed. Gethin had told me about the incident when he got home from school that day. But seeing him relive it again on the screen, all I wanted to do was make sure that Gethin was OK. Watching it on television really churned me up and upset me quite a bit. If Mr Michael had been nearby, he would have known exactly how upset I felt about it."

The three Griffiths children said that it was the change of language that was the most difficult adjustment for them. And this was a problem not only in the school (where the lessons were all in English, something which they were not used to in their schools in Cardigan), but also in their day-to-day lives. Speaking English at home with each other and their parents, for the cameras, was a completely new experience for the three of them.

* * *

But, for all five of them, the whole experience was a very special one, which has left its mark on them and still influences them even today, a few years down the line.

"I look at things differently now," says Debra. "When I came home after the filming, yes, it was nice to have an oven, a dishwasher and things like that. These days, if the oven is broken, I can go and get a Chinese takeaway. But having lived in circumstances where I knew that, if the fire went out, there would be no food for the family, well, that does change your outlook on all sorts of things. I appreciate things now that I used to take for granted."

"I'm extremely proud," says Cerdin, "of the way that my family coped with their various experiences in the Coal House. I could never have imagined that Debra would have been able to kill and prepare a rabbit or a hen, for example. The children went through massive changes, like speaking another language as well as adapting to a whole new way of living, and they did all this without complaining or protesting too much. They stayed happy throughout everything and that makes me very proud of them all indeed."

This book is just one of a whole range of publications from Y Lolfa. For a full list of books currently in print, send now for your free copy of our new full-colour catalogue. Or simply surf into our website

www.ylolfa.com

for secure on-line ordering.

TALYBONT CEREDIGION CYMRU SY24 5HE
e-mail ylolfa@ylolfa.com
website www.ylolfa.com
phone (01970) 832 304
fax 832 782